AF808490

THE NEW LAWYER'S

HIP-POCKET GUIDE TO APPEARING IN COURT

2D ED.

BY

MARC D. GARFINKLE, ESQ.

THE NEW LAWYER'S HIP-POCKET GUIDE TO APPEARING IN COURT

2D ED.

By Marc Garfinkle, Esq.

Hip-Pocket Guide Press, Inc.

2070 MILLBURN AVE.
MAPLEWOOD, NJ 07040
973-275-1313

ISBN-13: 9780984380176
ISBN-10: 0984380175

DISCOUNTS FOR
taxpayer-funded organizations,
US Military veterans and active duty personnel
Proudly printed in the USA

Dedicated to the lawyers
who teach other lawyers
to be better lawyers

?

Why This Guide?

Contrary to popular belief, attorneys are not born knowing how to handle court appearances any more than doctors are born knowing how to use a scalpel. Law school does not give us the tools nor teach us the techniques which enable us to excel when we go to court.

Your first appearance in court, much like your hundredth, may be guided only by what you've seen other lawyers do in court and on television, or what your own instinct tells you is good. In a sense, you are flying blind.

This little guide contains the ground rules. It should answer some questions, raise some *caveats* and offer some suggestions. It does not pretend to be exhaustive. Some experts will disagree with me.

This guide was conceived with the new lawyer in mind, but the information should serve even the most experienced attorneys. It draws on *my* experience, which is predominantly in trial courts with criminal matters and "simple" civil litigation, not "complex" litigation or federal court. Nonetheless, much of the advice here applies to courtrooms of every ilk.

All lawyers can improve their courtroom appearances and experiences by honoring a few simple practices. I describe them here briefly. Just by knowing how to "be" in court, you will appear the better lawyer and reap the benefits of that perception.

By refining your courtroom *persona,* you will create a better impression upon the judge, your adversaries and your clients. By respecting the dignity and solemnity of the courtroom and by honoring certain customs and conventions, you will lend added importance to being a courtroom lawyer.

M.D.G.

Ticket to Ride

Let's assume that you have received a notice advising that you, or your client, must appear in a certain court at a certain time. Unless you have a reliable GPS in your car, immediately get directions to the court and include a copy in your file.

If the court is a municipal court, ascertain that you have determined the correct municipality in order to avoid confusion with another municipality of same or similar name. Also, if the matter involves a summons issued by a police officer, the "date to appear" in court may not be a court day at all. It always pays to call the court to confirm.

You should also note all court appearances in your diary with a "tickler" the day before. Use this tickler to remind you to confirm your appearances for the following day (or Monday); don't count on courts to always notify you of schedule changes. Also, be sure to remind your client of the appearance.

If a client fails to appear in court, some judges require proof that the attorney notified the client in writing of the date. It is a good practice, even if not required. Email, if your client has it, is the best way to keep in touch about court dates and adjournments. Texting works well, too.

On The Road Again

Allow plenty of time to get to court. Whenever possible, avoid travelling to the court with your client. If your appearance is less than successful, few clients will be fun company on the drive back. It is far better to meet the client at the court.

Carry the judge's or the court's phone number with you on the file jacket or in your cell phone. Make sure your client has it, too. If either of you is stuck in traffic or otherwise going to be late, a simple call (hands-free, of course), will keep you off the judge's short list.

As Time Goes By

It is *usually* a good practice to be on time for court. Sometimes, punctuality will actually get you out earlier, too. As you gain familiarity, you may learn of particular courts or judges where attorneys need not appear until 10:00 as long as the client appears by 9:00, or where a phone call requesting a "ready hold" marking is acceptable.

These are often criminal courts, where one prosecutor will be in court for the entire session, or workers' compensation courts, where an insurance attorney may spend the entire session with one judge. Pay attention to the protocol in each court.

Judicious use of such information may save you countless hours over a long career, but don't plan on being late unless you are sure of the jurisdiction and the judge. Even in those courts where it's "okay" to be late, you should always call and leave word that you expect to be there at a certain time.

Blue Suede Shoes

Lawyers usually dress professionally. Clients often don't. Make sure your client knows how to dress. Attire should be professional. No hats, no sunglasses, no fancy jewelry, no sneakers or casual shoes. Although courts and counsel vary, it is never a *bad* idea for men to wear jackets and ties, and women to wear dresses, skirts or pantsuits. Some courts still discourage pantsuits for women. Imagine that!

Even where casual attire seems to be the rule, the nicely dressed party shows more respect to the court. You never know when that little edge may tip the scales in your favor. If you have any doubts about appropriate dress, call the court clerk or a lawyer who might know, beforehand.

Walk on By

Going through the metal detector is at the threshold of a courtroom experience. Most courts, particularly those that handle criminal cases, now have two metal detectors. One machine scans *objects* that are placed on a conveyor belt; a larger machine, adjacent, scans *people* as they pass through. Sometimes, a magnetic wand is used instead. In jurisdictions where attorneys are issued ID cards, have your Attorney Identification card available to find it quickly.

There is always at least one attorney who passes awkwardly through the metal detector, who repeatedly sets off a metal detector and doesn't know why. S/he looks amateurish to the client, and may engender ill will among the people, maybe even your jurors, waiting in line outside in the rain.

The best approach is to place all your metal objects, cigarette packs, keys, metal pens, cell phones, Blackberries, into the tray or dish provided for that purpose, or into a coat pocket or briefcase. The tray, coat or briefcase can then be passed through the machine which sees the contents. You can then walk through with grace.

Hello, Goodbye

It is a good habit to greet and chat with the court officer, the clerk, the prosecutor, and other court personnel, even when you are in a court that is new to you. You may well be back. People remember you, usually favorably, if you take a moment to acknowledge them and talk to them.

The dividends are subtle but rich. When you walk into a courtroom where you haven't been in months, and the officer at the metal detector greets you with a familiar, "Good morning counsel. How have you been?" you'll feel good, and your client will be impressed.

Don't Be Cruel

There is another important reason for you and your client to always be polite to the court staff: judges quickly hear of any perceived rudeness. You may have been entirely correct last week on the phone, and the court's staff may well have been inept, dishonest and evil.

Their stupidity may have cost you or your client time and money, their rudeness may have been shocking; but keep a civil tongue. More than a few judges have initiated an appearance by asking, "Was that *you* who spoke so rudely to my administrator, counsel?" There is no good answer.

<u>The Sounds of Silence</u>

Cell phones present most of the assaults on courtroom decorum. Signs at the doors advise people to turn off all cell phones in court. Usually, an officer or judge warns of harsh penalties for cell phones violations.

Still, there is almost always one person whose phone rings, usually with a ridiculous ringtone. You don't want to be that person. You don't want your client to be, either.

The best advice is to leave your cell phone in a briefcase or, even better, in the car. Much like the attorney who holds up the line at the metal detector, the attorney (or client) whose cell phone sounds during court will be disdained by everyone for the balance of the day. You can do without those bad vibes in court when your client's case is called.

We Have All Been Here, Before

If you are scheduled to appear in a court that you've never been to, or you are handling a matter that may be handled in a variety of ways, get the lay of land in advance. Do not be embarrassed to question other lawyers or the court clerk or a court officer.

It is better to plead ignorance to a colleague than to demonstrate it to a client. Learn all you can before you sit down in the courtroom. Lawyers are not like plastic surgeons who've patented a new procedure. We gladly share our trade secrets with even our newest colleagues. Take advantage of that!

Find someone who might know how the court, or this particular judge or prosecutor, handles the sort of matter you have. Ask whatever questions you have. You may learn valuable additional information, too. You may find out that you have at least an hour before the judge will hear you, that the Trooper is on vacation, or that you don't need to put more quarters in the parking meter after noon on court days. You may learn what kind of mood the prosecutor is in, or that the judge is in a hurry to get to his daughter's soccer game. Knowledge is power.

Yackety, Yack

No court appreciates "spectators" who converse while court is in session. Do not talk to your client or other lawyers in the courtroom. If you must speak, it is far better to leave the courtroom and discuss the matter in the hall. While seated in court, avoid reading any material, even your file, and do not send text messages from the court. Even if you see others doing so, say, before the judge comes out, ask the officer or clerk whether you may do likewise. Assume nothing.

Avoid appearing casual. Keep arms off the bench backs; both feet on the floor. Some courts reserve some seats in front for attorneys. You may choose to sit there or to stay with your client. Play it by ear. Just don't converse.

Help!!

If your client will be requiring an interpreter or a sign-language or hearing accommodation or if someone has a medical condition the court should know about, it is wise to advise a court officer or administrator at the earliest practical moment. If you don't, you may suffer unnecessary delay when your case is called.

The same principal applies to equipment such as screens, monitors or blackboards which you may require. Whenever possible, bring your own.

Jump!

Often the first impression a court will have is when your client's name is called at the roll call. Since we always stand when speaking to the court or when spoken to by the court, roll call is no exception. When your client's name is called, you should both stand and you should say, "Present with counsel," or "Ready for defendant," or however it is done there.

The court may not yet need to know who you are. That comes shortly.

Turn, Turn, Turn

Eventually, it will be *your* turn. If yours is not the first case, you should pay attention to how other counsel have approached counsel table. Since there are often two to or more approaches to the counsel area, plan the best approach. It is bad form to cross a courtroom between the judge and the public. If you must leave the courtroom or move to a different part of it while another matter is being heard, avoid walking in front of the judge, even if it means going around the entire courtroom.

You will stand when your case is called. As you stand, make sure that you are not disheveled. Men should quickly make sure that their shoes are tied, their suit jackets are buttoned and that their fly zippers are closed. Women should straighten their dresses or skirts.

Purses, backpacks or handbags should left at your seats when approaching. If this is impractical, look to the court officer or clerk to indicate where to place the bag.

Stand by Me

If yours is the first case called, you may not know where you should stand. In a courtroom with a jury box, the state or plaintiff usually takes the position closest to the jury. If you are at counsel table with a client, the client generally stands to your side which is farthest from the center. In other words, if you are on the left of center, the client is to your left; on the right, your client is to your right. Remain standing until the judge directs you to be seated. Stand with heels together and toes a bit apart, at "attention" but less rigid.

Keep your hands at your sides, so you may use them freely if you gesture. Using your hands expressively is appropriate, and may be persuasive, although in federal court or arguing appeals, it may be disfavored. Do not rock back and forth or hang on to the podium.

Under no circumstances should you or your client have hands in pockets. Few judges let this go unnoticed. It is not only inappropriately casual, but it may raise a security issue. Correct the situation before the judge or court officer does.

It should be obvious (but apparently it isn't) that chewing gum by clients or attorneys in the courtroom. Not only does gum-chewing obscure your speech, it does little to enhance the impression of intelligence that you and your client are trying to convey. Park your gum outside.

Who Are You?

Every court has a protocol for submitting a notice of your representation. They vary widely. If you have not submitted a written notice of representation with the court, or if you have only faxed one shortly before, it is a good idea to bring one with you to the court to offer at the time your case is called. Normally, the first thing a judge will say, once you are standing at counsel table or the podium is, "Appearances, please counsel" or "State you appearances for the record please."

In criminal cases, the prosecutor states his/her appearance first; in civil cases, the plaintiff generally does. In motion practice, the moving party or petitioner speaks before the answering party or respondent. When announcing your name, speak slowly and clearly. For some reason, lawyers race through their names as if they are embarrassed by them. All too often, an attorney announces his/her name at counsel table, and the clerk, the court reporter and other lawyers in the courtroom glance around to see if someone caught counsel's name. Take at least twice as much time to say your name as you normally would. Practice it a few times out loud. Even if it sounds funny to you, it will not sound funny in court.

When you "spell your last name for the record," particularly if your name is unusual or spelled in an atypical manner, spell it a half-speed, also. The court and the court staff will appreciate your assistance.

Stuck in the Middle with You

After you've stated your name and your firm's name, indicate your client's name and relationship to the matter. Introducing corporate clients or other business entities may require some verbiage at the front door. "Good afternoon, your Honor. I am Georgia Peach from the Law Offices of Bloom, Flowers and Dye, representing Joe's Hot Dogs, Inc. Frank Furter, Vice President of Operations for Joe's is present with me (optional: "at counsel table")(optional: "and standing to my right") (*very* optional: "which is the Court's left" – yuck!).

Courts are occasionally duped by imposters, so your client may be asked to provide proof of identity. Remind your client to bring ID.

Promises

Your client's (or witness's) testimony may require that s/he make an oath or affirmation. Explain to your client or witness in advance what that means. Courts cannot require that someone swear to God, so there is always the option for the witness to affirm, to state under penalty of perjury that the testimony will be true. Some court officers or judges forget to offer this option.

You should know in advance whether your witness will swear or affirm. When your non-swearing witness is instructed to raise the right hand and put the left hand on the bible, you may interrupt with, "She will affirm, thank you." Not a problem. They will ask her, "Do you affirm that the testimony..."

You Can't Sit Down!

You and your client should rise whenever the judge stands up or enters or leaves the courtroom. This is invariable unless the court or court officer directs that you remain seated. If, for any reason, you wish to remain seated during a proceeding where you would normally stand, ask the court for permission, directly: "Your Honor, may I remain seated during my examination of this witness? " Your request will rarely be denied.

Hey, You

The judge's name is "Your Honor," although you may refer to the judge as "the Court" or "the Bench." Never say "you" or "your" when addressing the court. You may see lawyers refer to the judge on the bench as "Judge." That is improper. "Judge" is the job description. "Your Honor" is the title. "Judge" is familiar. "Your Honor" and "the Bench" are the only appropriate ways to refer to a judge on the bench. You may call a judge, "Judge" in chambers, in the hallway, at a child's birthday party or at the supermarket. On the bench, however, the judge is always "Your Honor."

Your clients or witnesses who may be questioned by the judge should be instructed to say, "Yes, Your Honor," and, "No, Your Honor," etc., although it is not disrespectful for a lay person to refer to the Court as, "Sir" or "Ma'am.

Return to Sender

When before the court, *all* remarks are addressed to the court. Comments should never be directed toward opposing counsel or the client. We do not refer to our adversaries as "he" or "she," but we say "counsel" or "the prosecution." We rarely have reason to look in our adversary's direction.

Although we normally address the bench, the judge may direct us to do otherwise. For example, a judge might say, "Please elicit a factual basis from your client, counsel," meaning that the court is directing you to *voir dire* your own client on the record to establish that there is a legal basis for his/her guilty plea. It's normally far less stressful for you and your client to do it this way than to have the judge do it.

If your adversary addresses a remark to you directly (e.g."Well, did you bring the transcript with you?"), look directly at the court. You may ask, "Shall I respond, Your Honor?" If the court indicates that you are expected to respond, you should address the court, "Your Honor, I have (or don't have) the transcript with me in court today."

<u>You Can't Do That!</u>

If there is a cardinal rule, one even more sacrosanct than to stand when addressed by the court, it is that one should never interrupt the court.

When a judge cuts us off, there is a tendency to want to finish what we were saying. That is a dangerous tendency. Judges seem more irked by this particular *faux pas* than by almost any other breach of courtroom decorum.

Blue Moon

If there *is* a time when it *may* be acceptable for counsel to interrupt a speaking judge, it is when the judge has clearly misstated something or has made an incorrect assumption, and all counsel will agree that it was a misstatement or error. It is never easy to be the one who stops the judge, although the judge may prove to be appreciative.

One way to do that is to stand up and await acknowledgement. That failing, you might risk saying, "If I may, your Honor…" or "May it please the Court…." and see whether you are acknowledged. If so, you should delicately state your thought, and hope that other counsel are nodding in agreement. If not, be prepared for a judge whose thoughts will run toward decapitation.

I Can't Get No Satisfaction

Wrath might also rain upon a lawyer who, upset by a court's ruling, leaves counsel table with a clearly displeased countenance. Some attorneys (and more than a few clients) even mutter displeasure as they leave the judge's earshot, or gripe sorely to colleagues in the hall. Never underestimate the loyalty of the "regulars" or the sensitivity of a courtroom recording system. And the Ethics Committee won't take lightly a lawyer's affront to the court. Suck it up and smile.

Please Don't Let Me Be Misunderstood

Courtroom language, when addressing the court or counsel, should be more formal than language you use elsewhere. You need not speak Elizabethan English, but a rich vocabulary is always appropriate. Select good words. Employ clear diction. But pay attention to local custom and practice. Sometimes, smart and polished is just the WRONG style for the court you are in.

While it is usually good to appear a tad more erudite than the other players in the sandbox, there will also be times when you will want to temper your courtroom *persona* to avoid looking too different, particularly in a court that's new to you.

Your client wants to see that you fit in. So, fit in. When in Rome....

Please Please Me

Some attorneys are comfortable prefacing their comments with a formal tag line such as, "May it please the court..." Some attorneys are uncomfortable with such relics in our professional jargon. If you can use this language comfortably, and not overuse it, then it can be impressive.

Whenever possible, comments to the court should be in the passive voice, as long as they don't sound silly. For example, it is better form to say, "May I be heard?" than "May I speak?" We say, "May I be heard as to sentencing, your Honor?" or "May I be heard at sidebar?" We seek "leave" not permission, to do something, may it please the court. And we always thank the court at the end.

You Don't Own Me!

Avoid calling your client "my client." That connotes a cold business relationship and reduces your client to a check-signer. Worse, each time you refer to your client as "my client", you are losing an opportunity to give that person or business a more sympathetic or memorable label. Refer to your clients by their roles (e.g., plaintiff, moving party, petitioner, respondent), or by name, where appropriate (e.g., Mr. Jones or Ms. Smith). Throw in adjectives or modifiers when fitting.

Never use first names. It is informal. If you wish to use first names for, say, a child, ask the court's permission to refer to that person by first name only. Use may use BOTH names, if you wish. "Your Honor: Mr. Smith, (his many friends call him 'Ollie', your Honor) has expressed remorse, etc."

Humanize your client, even if your client isn't human. "MegaCorp, which employs hundreds of our friends and neighbors, asks your Honor…." A sympathetic label can be a powerful tool in court.

Doo Wah Diddy Diddy

Saying "my client" is bad enough, but at least it is grammatically correct. Some horrible usages surface in court time and again; I warn you here against them.

"Complaintant" with two "Ts" is not a word. "Complainant" with one "T" is.

Nothing is *"unequivocable"* or "unequivocably;" something may be "unequivocal" or "unequivocally."

"Irregardless" is not a word. It is a hybrid of "irrespective" and "regardless."

"As of yet" must mean "as of now", I suppose. Maybe it just means "yet." You decide.

"Unique" means "one of a kind." Nothing can be *"very unique"* or *"somewhat unique"*.

"Past experience" and *"prior history"* are redundant.

A *verbal* warning means that words were you. An oral warning means the words were spoken.

Do You Want to Know a Secret?

Sometimes, we wish to ask the judge a question or discuss a particular matter with the judge, but only in the presence of the judge and other counsel. To request a sidebar conference, such as to ask the court for a preemptive ruling or to avoid saying something privileged in open court, we ask the court to hear us at sidebar. Sidebar discussions are on the record, but out of the earshot of the public, the witness or the jury.

Every Picture Tells a Story

Sometimes, we must hand something to the judge or receive something the judge is offering, usually a document. When this happens, look to the court officer. Normally, the officer will take the document from you and give it to the court, and vice versa. Don't for get to say, "Thank you."

Even in courts where it is clear that you may do so personally, or that the officer is unavailable, you should always request the court's permission to approach the bench. The usual way to do this is to ask, "Your Honor, may I approach the Bench?" or simply, "May I approach?" This time-honored custom echoes historical concerns for the judge's safety, and all judges appreciate this courtesy, even if the custom is more honored in the breach than in the observance.

The Letter

There will be times when you wish to present evidence. Tangible evidence is submitted in the form of exhibits (as opposed to testimony). If the evidence is documentary, bring at least four copies with you - one each for you, the witness, your adversary and the court. Try to learn whether the judge prefers counsel to pre-mark exhibits. You'll want to go with the flow.

Never allow your witness to take the witness stand with papers or files in his/her hand. Many courts will allow your adversary to examine all papers brought by the witness to the stand. This can open a Pandora's Box of discovery, privilege and other issues which could have been avoided. If your witness approaches the witness stand with papers or files in hand, you should offer, "Here, let me hold those papers for you, before you take the stand."

Put on a Happy Face

When a judge makes a ruling, however unfavorable, it is usually appropriate to thank the court for ruling. We are not indicating our pleasure or agreement with the ruling. It may help to explain this to a client *before* she sees you thank a judge for a ruling that goes the wrong way.

Of course, if the judge orders your client to jail, you might consider a different approach.

When a matter is concluded, you should always say, "Thank you, your Honor." When appropriate, it is also nice to thank opposing counsel ("Thank you, counsel," or "Thank you, Ms. Jones") or thank a particularly helpful clerk or officer. They will remember.

Run For Your Life, If You Can

If you should be so fortunate as to have a judge dismiss a case against your client because a witness or party is not present, you and your client should leave the court immediately. If there is an elevator, take the stairs.

Every lawyer knows a story about a "dismissed" defendant who bumps into the other party just as the defendant is leaving the courtroom or the elevator. The judge recalls the case, and the beat goes on. It's better to tell the story about someone else.

The Way You Do The Things You Do

Most lawyers wear many hats, play many roles, and serve many functions. Yet, of all that we do, representing a party in court is our highest calling. *Courtrooms* are where our society's values are defined and our government's policies are tested. Courtrooms are where our bitterest disputes are resolved and our notion of justice is made manifest.

Whose voice but a lawyer's should echo "Objection!" from marble walls when untrustworthy evidence is being offered in a cause? Who but a lawyer should explain a situation so that a judge understands it the right way? Lawyers in court are like MDs in surgery...no one else should be doing it.

Effective courtroom advocacy is the capstone skill for lawyers. When you fully understand what it means to be an advocate, to be the mouthpiece, to be the sword or shield of a formerly unrepresented person or entity, you will better appreciate your time in court. See you there.

MDG

Marc Garfinkle is a lawyer with over thirty years of criminal and civil trial experience. He lives in New Jersey with his wife, Eylana.

In addition to his practice, Marc is Adjunct Professor of Persuasion and Advocacy at Seton Hall University Law School and is Public Defender in lovely suburban Livingston, NJ. He teaches skills for the National Institute of Trial Advocacy (NITA), provides continuing legal education to lawyers, and is a featured faculty member of Lawline.com.

A former chair of the N.J. Supreme Court District (VB) Attorney Ethics Committee, he is a member of Phi Beta Kappa, the American Bar Association, the Association for Continuing Legal Education (ACLEA), the Association of Criminal Defense Lawyers, and the N.J. Association for Justice.

Marc has also written *"$olo Contendere: How to Go Directly from Law School into the Practice of Law Without Getting a Job,"* and several other *Hip-Pocket Guides.*

Made in United States
Troutdale, OR
11/03/2026

56852527R00024